Flesh, A Naked Dress

Susan Andrews Grace

HAGIOS PRESS
Box 33024 Cathedral PO
Regina SK S4T 7X2

Library and Archives Canada Cataloguing in Publication

Grace, Susan Andrews, 1949-
    Flesh, a naked dress / Susan Andrews Grace.

Poems.
ISBN 0-9739727-1-8

    I. Title.

PS8563.R31F54 2006   C811'.54   C2006-901929-0

Edited by Hilary Clark.
Designed and typeset by Donald Ward.
Cover artwork: *Tree* (collagraph print) by Natasha Smith.
Cover design by Yves Noblet.
Set in Adobe Caslon.
Printed and bound in Canada at Houghton Boston Printers & Lithographers, Saskatoon.

The publishers gratefully acknowledge the assistance of the Saskatchewan Arts Board, The Canada Council for the Arts, and the Cultural Industries Development Fund (Saskatchewan Department of Culture, Youth & Recreation) in the production of this book.

Flesh, A Naked Dress

HAGIOS PRESS

Acknowledgements

Thanks to the Saskatchewan Arts Board for a grant that allowed me time to write some of these poems. Thanks also to Professors Claudia Keelan, Doug Unger, Dave Hickey, and Richard Wiley of the University of Nevada, Las Vegas, for their reading of some of this work. Many thanks to Joyce MacDonald for her editorial suggestions and to Laurel Glitherow, Bobbie Ogletree, Paige Adair, Jennifer Craig, Nicola Harwood, Jana Danniels, and Verna Relkoff for wise counsel. I would like to acknowledge Eileen Delehanty Pearkes's *The Geography of Memory: Recovering Stories of a Landscape's First People,* which guided the writing of "Erasmus in the Kootenays" with eloquence and sureness. Thank you, Sylvia Legris, for the phone calls which kept me on track.

Excerpts from these works, sometimes in earlier versions, have appeared in the following periodicals and one anthology:

"Flesh, A Naked Dress" in *Canadian Literature;*

"Luther in the Desert" in *Horsefly;*

"A Sometime Gravity" in *In Medias Res* and *Poetry Nottingham International;*

"Joy of the Proper Tool" in *Other Voices: Journal of the Literary & Visual Arts* and *Listening with the Ear of the Heart* (edited by Dave Margoshes and Shelley Sopher).

Contents

Geography is simply a visible form of theology.

Jon D. Levenson
Sinai and Zion

The flesh and all that is formed out of the blood into flesh show the soul within.

Plotinus
The Enneads VI.4.9

Erasmus in the Kootenays

But meanwhile certain pedants raise a clamour, eager
to pierce, as if they were crows, the eyes of theologians,
covering with their annotations, as with smoke, the
commentaries of others. Of this group I would mention,
by way of honour, Erasmus. For if he doesn't stand in
first place, he is certainly in second. What a foolish
citation, worthy of Folly.

Erasmus
The Praise of Folly

I quickly spat it out, prompted by a belief that
something tasting that bitter might be poisonous.
But the soopallalie is no more poisonous than sorrow.
Embarrassed at my lack of courage, I popped another
into my mouth, trying to allow for the sharp, acrid juice
to roll wildly on my tongue.... Bitterness is a tonic for
the heart, I have been told.

Eileen Delehanty Pearkes
The Geography of Memory

In this Life One Must Be On Guard

So you say, Erasmus. There are other ways
to fight the Adam and Eve in us, with that handy little weapon,
    the *enchiridion*,
a dagger against Folly to whom you otherwhere sing praises.
There's nothing like the weapon of shame to shade
difference: many definitions, you said, lead to shame.
Here in wet montane forests: cedar, hemlock, fir, pine and larch
shade secrets too. Where does God reside?
You'll love this, Erasmus: it's rich:
all trace of human and divine erased. Here in the Kootenays
two, maybe three, generations of memory.

On the Thinly Disguised Incident Involving
Thomas More and Dame Alice More

Who's to believe you Erasmus, writing of such tomfoolery as
the fool who was a FoolishTom, not a Tom Fool, and tricked
his wife with false jewels. The wife was satisfied, nevertheless,
thinking them real and that her husband did love her. She the
Fooled or he the Fool, one wonders and who is the virtuous
and what about Adam and Eve.

Paternity's Question

In the Kootenays there is hidden trace of the forebears. A thief
stole the jewels in the bright light of Christian day with a
    levelling plough,
made fake feminine of the land. There were priests here too
and probably fathered children like you under the lodgepoles
and woven reed roofs, they left the mothers. It happened
    everywhere:
in your world, and this world of isolated valleys and roaring
    waterfalls:
Adams and Eves, Fools and Dames.

If-Only

Oh the indigo and scarlet jewels here, Erasmus!
Blueberries, huckleberries, currants, and gooseberries,
raspberries and wild cherries: the people believed in folly
and called him Coyote and all enjoyed the fruit.
Now a coyote can be seen on the streets of Nelson,
looking for the trick. The buried remains of folly
flooded, baptized by hydroelectric reservoirs. If only
you'd been here to mock the friars of engineering.
Four hundred years after your failure, your blending
belief and courage, ancient wisdom might have saved
the wild water: priests and seminarians complicit.

How could you, Erasmus!

The most thoroughly happy is the most thoroughly deluded
you said. And kings are most unhappy and most avoid
wise men for fear they speak truth except
they should disguise it as foolery. You had none of More's
   percipience.
More who knew the King's defence, who bled sweat and
   epithets to Luther
knowing the split to come: revolution: but still he followed
fate to the gallows: the church in two: his body and head
in leave-taking. Two pages of *Moirae Encomium*,
The Praise of Folly, pre-wrote his life. More's the pity
you couldn't have foreseen and forewarned the bloody end too.
And you the intellectual titan: such foolery.

He lost his head, in reality the end of his neck lost
More, he lost his head over losing his head over
Luther and the King and you wrote, even dedicated the book
   to him,
he who would have no defence but the truth.

Erasmus, the wise man hiding behind Folly's skirts, I invite you,
your witty spirit in scrubbed Rotterdam, to enjoy the
Kootenays.
                     It's a thing that Horace's Greek might call sanity:
applauding invisible drama on an empty stage with haunted
   pleasure.
Welcome to the archaeological amphitheatre of late antiquity
in Slocan, along the shores of Arrow Lakes, at Galena Bay.
Laugh or cry: we're not sure which traces wash away,
heaped fluvial middens at false shorelines:
flooded for power.

Demons are those who know

And yet Folly's wisdom is that of a woman looking for trouble
in grammars and letters. Even the saints, you said, were stupid,
cowards and thieves as they survived disaster, poisonings,
adultery to the Church's profit. Starving wonder at starspill
  over heaven
keeps theologians and scientists scratching at fleas and lice
while doctors and lawyers fleece the faithful.

Folly Laughs at the Bishop

Folly chastises the Bishop, soiled by insincerity, his ignorance
   of balance
between Hebrew and Christian law, a two-horned mitre.
The Bishop prances behind the cross, Folly says,
ignoring his vow against carnal affection, lustily
tripping the pretty boys: he has frocked and gloved his filth.

In Kootenay villages in spring, long before Jesus
began the life of one law, starved processions laced through the
   houses
when new shoots shot up in the rock clefts,
                        deer descended the mountain to eat
men danced out and women clapped in, cleansing their bodies.

Pretensions

When women weave space, there's not the same room for Folly —
ovals of birch, inside out bark, pitched and sealed for cooking,
highest living. There's no pretending to strength,
fingers bend cottonwood or they don't: baskets to carry fish
from shore to fire. Folly's a false god if she cannot feed you.

And you Erasmus, who used your intelligence to pierce hypocrisy
like a poorly-made basket and leak its self-indulgence
how you might have loved this place:

                              its cleanliness
and its people who lived in pristine mind on the wild water
square keels piercing waves, no time for posturing.
Time shone on days, slept at night
and stretched into hours of rain.

Erythronium Grandiflorum

A grizzly bear digs up the yellow glacier lily, its petals
turned back onto delicacy, defenceless.
Days later the grizzly returns to eat the root, knows
it has turned sweet while he is away.

As if drunkenness and fornication were worthy of capital
   punishment,
theologians, your colleagues, Erasmus quibbled, then ignored
   indolence and
made witches of Christ's most holy. At the same time were
   people
who knew what the grizzly did, those who used swords of wit
   and honesty
against the farting friar, those who held the purse of lettuce
seed in their apron pockets,
and the stupid lamb who bawled at every village door
his mother lost in a moonless night.
                              God's sun came in morning
to save the lamb, as long as the theologians were away.
                              And you Erasmus
noticed it all, defenceless as a lily to stop it.

Erasmus, had the people here stayed lost in the moon, never
   seen God's sun
borrowed by Christians who considered themselves greater
   than Christ, they would
have been saved. But God's sun was brought here.

        The avalanche lily still clings to the slope. It makes
no difference to the lily or the sparrow what we've done
or not done, a chasm of forgetting
swallows the trace.

Blue Elderberry

A sense of place: Rotterdam or the Kootenays, water or land
heaven or hell: Did you, Erasmus, ever consider blue
as a place: sky or water or elderberry?
Nothing is forgiven wisdom in heaven, only foolishness
gets away with everything:
the fishermen, women and children whom Jesus loved
lived here for millennia: harvested a plain of blue
lived under another. Even the insides of their cedar root
  baskets
were rubbed blue, water-proofed with elderberry.
What might you have written, how might your
heart have healed had you portaged around Bonnington Falls,
waxy berries to your right as you breathed in the mist
surrounded by a wild God.

Kinnickkinnick

Since the glacier melt and shadows in Greek caves
and the perfect madness of perfect love
the fast is a fact of human life.
Spring's salvation, natural fast,
renews the body of the already-well,
steals breath

time's most holy possession, from old people, sickly children,
post-parturient women, the fools of all time
in any time, those submerged in life's
extremity and those who die of the fast.
But you spoke of a different, religious fast.

In the time of Salish subterranean pit houses
and in your sixteenth century cobbled life
the same rules of nourishment: food or no-food.
You said the soul needs a fast from pride and anger.
The well-fed soul, I presume.

If you'd been a Kootenay faster, Erasmus,
I wager you'd have been much happier
            : long months of story telling to replace Advent,
                  Christmas, Lent
            : winter dances, visions and dreams
            in night's prosperous trapping territory,
            hammered kinnickkinnick berries for hosts
            salmon eggs for wine
            : pristine ceremony to break fast.

Joy of the Proper Tool

Fasts and vigils, the study of Scripture, renouncing
possessions and everything worldly are not in themselves
perfection, as we have said; they are its tools. For
perfection is not to be found in them; it is acquired
through them.

St. John Cassian, quoting Abba Moses

We shape our tools and afterwards our tools shape us.

Marshall McLuhan

1

Eye of hawk
mouse.

Fecund earth
fetid water.

Fucking asshole
in a city: non-

identity, God's tool
perfect.

2

Newly-dead monks buried,
their work undone & agendas

underground with them.
The maze goes unmowed.

Chickadees chitter in the pines and spruce,
alight on blue-green looking for a Francis.

Dusk as time bullies
Benedictine magpies.

3

Eyeglasses bring the page home.
Sight sharpens. Awake!

Awake & listen: pages
and pages of grasses ahead:

plains, purple alfalfa
green wheat taking over

from fescue: wilderness
now weather.

4

God's palm opens to receive
foolish effort perfect tools.

How to learn not to pick and choose:
listen to the South Dakota boy who says

at a farewell party near the airport
the Dakotas are a lot of nothing:

Sunday mornings people go to church
then out for caramel buns at the café

admire the neighbour's daughter's baby, go home
drive through grasses.

Flesh, A Naked Dress

5

God's roughhousing: that homeless man —
a shame he is shitting on Decatur Boulevard,

openly like that — but he can't
use the toilet at the ARCO gas station.

O tool me a story, a drive
over to crazy

away from blunder: the perfect way.
Radio me in.

6

Life is round and blue
precious space:
                    home and refuge
                    nests in sky's wooden arms.

Spruce trees listen to stories
shroud closer

a man lost in the forest not homeless
no matter how naked.

7

Cholla and creosote bush punctuate
fierce desert

language
cicadas sing.

8

Now is a pale blue truck,
rusty, rattling

along the dusty road
unable

to complete
the trip.

Love a hollow oval
holy air

Siberian elm pushing up
green, wild praise.

Flesh, A Naked Dress

9

Buffalo bones ground
into china cups:

wilderness.
Buffalo were wild.

  *

Wilderness is north
wild + *deer* with racks big as

a bear's reach
silent.

10

Gravity holds (it's a handy tool)
gas in the bottom of the rusty tank

hole in the top half
sloshes gas & fumes

these free-trade roads
also full of holes

a radio like me
at once empty and full

picks up the whine
of the motor.

Now you see how wrong:
turn the corner

       unlikely larch,
cedar maze leads to a clearing

the hermit's house, tiny glade
its yellow perfection,
undone.

Nature's so often like this gap
unthinking itself, moving along

self-forgetful: short-term.
Glaciers missed the Cypress Hills

bristle cone pines, beachy things —
sand, gravel and shells up there.

12

Cactusquick pricks
prairie conscience

soft grasses heal, their sword-tips
soothed by wind.

    *

Drink whiskey out of tea cups
wine out of tumblers.

    *

Crows caw a mottled sky
leaf-lace wings the blues.

    *

Sun flattens heartache given to prayer:

       pray for holy endings

       pray for wise beginnings.

13

The plain is the sentiment that exalts us

pushes blooded exaltation
perfect pump for oxygen.

Radio me in, said Jack
pick me up into radio's pump

shoot me quickly through heaven
and then quick back to California.

Radio pumps in Outside and
stars, on the plain's roof

the firmament a spill of milk
across night. The heart

spits and pours and breaks
open, stays without perfection.

Mystery a lie told as if
we never die.

14

Was it right to surrender
language as if it mattered: it did: red

passages inhabited by daimons,
whispered Plotinus, you are lucky:

stars spill consciousness
in a desert evening: warm and dry

heals sinfulness, opens nightscents, delicate
and serried, infinite as the plains.

15

Lay out that intricately woven life,
its warp necessity, its weft circumstance:
permeability
is like that: relentless in the way it argues
unto death, undoes a white silk ribbon
unfurling its narrow good.

16

Mistakes! Look to the jimson flower
          its shocking tawdriness
roadside vaginal throat
open
          waves its panties at you
                    as you drive by
                    not making mistakes.

17

Lies in a state of betweenness:

fabrication but not to honour Fabricius

for whom mud is the dust of water. These lies

are spittle of the gods of houses, home,

repeated transition made by blood.

Accusation at its oaken doorway.

18

A sweater of greenness,
wear its blessed arms
to reach around
what's left.

19

Whatever it takes is what:
clouds shaped like flying saucers
cranes woven in red silk shoes
fat and good spectres, witches' knots
lilacs sick with longing
the grasses of Parnassus
are what it takes
grosgrain winceyette nainsook
jacquard paisley stockingette jersey
duffel nankeen corduroy
twill & moleskin dimity sharkskin
calico taffeta and moiré: foreskin —

as with all goodness, cloth leads the way.

20

Time to sing the psalms, their wraiths' smoky chant.
A chicken killed by a fox, on the path to the water. Dawn

has been an hour already, the chicken's neck collapsed,
feathers clumped by blood and scattered.

Don't look closely: you see nature better
from the corner of your eye.

21

Lies truth tells self-righteousness:

backward weaving.

Perfection is now's

rusty truck rattling down the pot-holed highway.

Flesh, A Naked Dress

A Sometime Gravity – Thomas More

As time requireth, a man of marvellous mirth and pastimes, and sometimes of as sad gravity, as who say: a man for all seasons.

Robert Whittington

Sir Thomas More, Knight sometime Lord Chancellor of England, a man of singular virtue and of a clear unspotted conscience, (as witnesseth Erasmus), more pure and white than the whitest snow, and of such an angelical wit, as England, he saith, never had the like before, nor never shall again, universally. . . .

William Roper

— What shifts under the rug is still under
the tightly woven wool of enclosures, poverty, excess
vanities swollen in the worst citizens.
The wise man steers clear of government

He will write the new law inwardly by the finger of God
on the book of the heart.

Tablets broken by fathers crumble and spin
into desert pavement long
before holy books. Still what God
wreaks upon the heart
lasts long.

Pride in Germany as in England
vainglory, buffoonery same in desert or forest.

      Dream your heart *Thomas Morus*:
              old woman guardian of the gate mocks
              crouches, laughs hard. Mythras waits
              underground.

Aut Erasmus, Aut Nullus

Folly is a woman: folly be praised. A man takes a wife,
    educates a daughter, obeys
the king, sings his Lord's supper, and a cadaverous monk calls
    him the very devil:
the Virgin Mary does not, he said, sit up late eternity
for sinners who recite her Psalter every day.

Folly is a woman. Folly has never seen such virtue: Erasmus
    hasn't either:
believes no monk resists seduction. Chastity a big hairy deal:
    God in a cucumber.
All monks are stupid Folly says. She speaks for Erasmus,
    praises Morus, Christ's fool.
Monks are less holy than the ass upon which Jesus sailed into
    Jerusalem.
Aristotelian dialectic up the ass's ass, Folly says.

Folly is a woman and she doesn't need to know
about God. She knows God. Folly has never been so beguiled:
    Moriae Encomium.
A man, used to Folly, used in fun by Erasmus, a man whose
    heart wrote
a rivulet of law: lust's inward bleeding: cold desert.

Viva Las Vegas or *A New Donatism* or *Perhaps He Has
Seen It in Utopia*, said More

When two or more are gathered to exclude someone from
  Christ's church
mad heretics buzz, desert schism blooms lusty gallant flowers
bright as self-mockery in spite of sun's rulership of the fourth
  century Donatist
North African desert, the fallen-away Mojave.
                        More, the playful bettor, lays his hand down:
Luther will extract not only Rome, but all of Italy, Germany,
  Spain, France, Britain,
holy orders blood of the new —
no counter to the devil's election in scripture's tyranny.
Traditio truth in our midst said More, who is lover of Lucian's lies
more than any other lies on earth
convicts Luther a liar and

———————————————

how could a Utopian — of Nowhere, England — know
      this puritan neon desert Luther founded by faith in
        salvation's nowhereness:
      its bloodless plastic ambition, fruit eyes in Caesar's Palace
      blinking sevens.

Flesh, A Naked Dress

The Gates of Hell

In the first hell are heresies: schism its gates. And so I say in the first place dismantling its bars is to threaten a king, leaving the way to hell open.

       Hair shirt, More's gates of hell are his repentance.
The King's gates not the King's to guard —
Luther's assurance Christ will prevail against the gates.
More's railings humiliation enough, gates *do not signify the devil* —
hair shirt, monkey suit — *for the gates of a house are not the*
  same as its master,
masters are not in control of their gates
nor are the gates of hell the same as the devil.

Or all is a dream from which
there will be no waking

———————————

unto the forgiveness

Unbridled Freedom of Saint Luther

I am not at all surprised if he has no fear of purgatory.

This friend of Paul needs nothing but excuses
from sins. Fashioning himself as Saint
Luther if you don't mind. And in the 21st century
  one has to wonder
in a desert rich in paradox, what was Morus
doing? Works without faith and faith without works
two sides   same coin   common
          wealth
Luther   Paul
                    Luther   More
          Paul   Morus
                    Luder   Satan   Lucifer

_____

                    And   upon   this

The King Defends Good Works or
The Neglect of Good Works by Luther

Though he does not require our good works, we do not sin
since He is God, we are not sparrows in the generosity of God's
  blue sky
and *without whose care not even one* of us requires impunity
  from sinning
and sparrows do not need healing earth
sparrows do triumph
                not even one sparrow falls to the earth,
        of which two
sparrows stay in their sky
two are sold
a sparrow a farthing
for two farthings
evil works cause no harm.
                      If only Luther knew conscience,
sin in England: holy men nowhere and anywhere
sparrows everywhere. More knows —

English Majesty Pelted with Shit

Come do not rage so violently, good father; but if you have raved
wildly enough, listen now, you pimp.
He who points a finger is not necessarily not what he points to.
Conscience is a she-wolf in a yellow kirtle
her bodice winks flesh and holy men
her keepers at winter's crossroads.

Flesh, A Naked Dress

The Holy Spirit Presides Over the Church

At supper or rather after supper Luther we need to know —
the King most especially wants to know — when will the Holy
   Spirit join
and all the faithful *Father Tosspot is always drunk*
and never the King *very early in the morning* is fasting *therefore*
never the King fabricates and Luther lies *no one can receive the
   sacrament*
soberly except in the morning. The Holy Spirit would like to
   come to
communion at supper or after supper —
she does not care. No books at the table.

See, reader, how ever he is like himself?

The Mass Anterior to the Gospels

This is the custom: *Do this in remembrance.*
He and Erasmus were their own fathers. *This is my body.*
Why not wash it? And my feet?
By what scripture could you avoid this?
Luther's sacraments only Baptism and the Eucharist
only those two
and the King's sacraments are seven
in his counting church
he is the richer
and will defend this confession, confirmation, marriage, holy
  orders, extreme unction —

More is left to the Mass
gospel good news
      the day after
      death's estrangement.

Auctoritas vs. Traditio

Augustine who said —
> *I would not believe the gospel unless the authority of the*
> *church did not persuade me.*

would likely confess nothing, fall into Luther's trap:
Luther knows the difference between papism and his invisible
  church for holy men, a club
Augustine most likely could not join: the true church
to judge doctrine, gospels, fire's beginning. More's ending
mutable, power the King's.

A red-tailed hawk sweeps summer fog
over More's New Building morning
glories blue the brambles, Friday climbs time.

  *

Inside
reeds freshly laid on the floor
eastern light glances
certain grace.

Flesh, A Naked Dress

Flesh, A Naked Dress

Every soul is, and becomes, that which she contemplates.

Plotinus
The Enneads IV.3.8

The seductive, ambivalent landscape of the half-seen
mountain — able to be read but not read, provoking as
much confusion as it does insight — is a metaphor of
the effort to speak of God.

Belden C. Lane
The Solace of Fierce Landscapes

The soul loves the good because from the beginning, she
has been incited by the Good to love him.

Plotinus
The Enneads VI.7.31

The perfect tool shoots utterly clean —

mulberry shoots tied against failure.

The cosmic mixing bowl

sound circles round.

Broken wing mended —

tinctures of music.

Something is gone forever, yet

communion is desert bright.

The bowl tips —

     as above circles

     so below traffic.

Orogenesis of these mountains:
vermilion blankets dropped behind hugely opened

doors — squeezed, bent, wrapped and broken.
The drive toward Paradise

down Sunset.
This day you shall be with me.

The desert burns
rock black with its varnish

a grapevine canyon waits
for a curled herd of sheep.

Inside airplanes
ascending souls

cherish earth,
paradise.

Flesh, A Naked Dress

Oh, in California
where it must be God loves more and better

purple morning glory holds
the white wall

flower-delicate necks push
heart leaves

half arcs
sharpened chiaroscuro.

It's easy when you've self-righteously scraped ice from
   windshields
brushed thick layers of snow from the roof
letting wind take care of the rest, to think

Californians only think God loves them more
but when you go to California via the near Arctic
and see bright pink strumpet flowers

climb a corner wall
and night-flowering jasmine wafts the evening away
you know, finally, God

is a miserable bastard or it would be jasmine everywhere.
And because of that thought you know
God will banish you from California.

Flesh, A Naked Dress

Sands and nakedness would be misunderstood by passers-by
as he shat on Decatur Boulevard, the desert father in search of
  adiaphoria

starvation accompanied by ravenous greed
and temptation to know.

Scientia falls
trapped by a web

bluish light, anonymous televisions.

Greed in famine-ridden worlds is different.
This mere velleity: daydreams of a homeless monk

on Decatur, facing white tigers
escaped and hungry. The soul cannot answer questions

his indignity asks, her purpose in a body, starved
and burned by sun. She's no good with tigers either.

A holy man could take the thorn from a large cat's paw
and receive loyalty forever, but that is a man's story,

man's God, and man's desert. She must deal with this
braid of rivers, real and unwet. She's what goes

back and forth. She's him, she's sun
she's not him, leaves often.

Flesh, A Naked Dress

Where feasts rise high
oranges, their leaves and green peppers

ruched tablecloths from a linen supply:
people hunger:

something green from a sinning God tempts
withholding and she must be here.

It's her job to chastise God.

Someone else sins in paradise.
Stone picked up, ready to pitch

from a wall of precision, at God.
Stone nestled into stone, balanced

art of ancestors:
holy blunders in a field

urged through the mantle to crust —
earth's confession.

Flesh, A Naked Dress

In the gleaming house she sings *Monte Circeo*
the walls' thick plaster smooth as cut flour

waxy grace of laurel and rosemary outside,
thick and thin shadow, blue flowers shy in deep foliage.

Her feet are bare
dusty sandals on the marble, door

          open
to birds who sing back.

     *

It does seem too perfect, the day not likely
to live up to itself, she lets it go on untouched

by her singing, summer fog rolling in.
The island hers alone, she sails

to the mainland when she must.

As prisons are temporary
she is a guest

whether she needs food
or not: three meals a day

in a strange land, succulence
an invention of hunger.

This is not a portion
it is one.

The Good knows that she, the soul, wants out but
it's not something he can help

he can't think her out
soul wears her heavy prison.

Muscles wrap bone, dendrite trees,
branches synapse-crazy, laced

capillaries: organic mystery. Eyes in another
holey space

mortal thought
self-conscious, blue-eyed:

the desert
will not let go of her tongue

its spiny succulence, thick water-holding flesh,
loves her fluency, flattening it

into bayonet cacti, round
sound rolls out.

Flesh, a naked dress —
tissues sewn with bloody threads

swims in air, frantic
sinks and gives back to the sun

dry drowning. All flesh
is as grass

wildflower wool
burdened overlay.

Pain splints pleasure

around soul's desert bed:
air filled with four o'clock's perfume

red purpure stakes her
arms and legs tied to clouts.

Driven deep into desert pavement
aeolian force over water and time

air's density less than water or ice
a blessing. She is made of infinity's

particles and coheres, presents
a smooth surface to the wind.

She is a Joshua tree, parched
in fierce wind
          its red root ends
spidery trace
on the desert floor.

She leaves the mountain
in a flurry of clothing: the Good

is her ethereal casing,
her idea of here.

Her feet cut by cinders from
a burnt century

remind her
she is without All and One.

He will get into the boat and
she will wave to him from the sky,

impeccably naked.

Oh, don't worry, Soul is a lake
blue and weak and Good is

a mountain of heaven. He can take her ascent
as he shelters his eyes with his forearm

to watch her. Good is treading water, holding
his mirror, her perfect conduct. And she

makes her tent in the space a lake takes
clouts anchored to something fiery.

A tiger wilts with thirst at the forest threshold.
A stumbly desert father may soon come over

the delicious embankment
bring water to the tiger.

She can see all this from her place.

This all takes place below the desert

and behind the tiger.

A horse and wagon trudge through the talus
not to the rise, not at the beginning yet.

She can see this. He cannot — he's looking at her.
He can see the thunder clouds piling up behind

her ascent — she cannot. The Good is a wagoner and wonders
at all sentient beings: the grasshopper's copper body,

the tiger, the man. The wagoner sees her in the sky
thunder clouds behind her and says to himself: "Bloody Hell

how did she do that?" and urges his horse into
the difficult footing of a fallen mountain.

Thunder's presence joyful prescience
sky splits open. The horse breaks away
failure laden with a wagon, a desire to see her

come down. She's wet and shaken by the terrible.

A blade of grass struggles to sprout
against an obstacle
a broken blue tea cup, buried.

If she can make it, she thinks to herself, she will wait

five decades. Enough to push aside, grow
around this earthy blue curve.

Five decades and the wagoner, his wagon,
and horse are horizon.

Thunder and lightning success.

She has an abundance or wetness
which dries often and returns to the clear desert below.

The tiger circles the region with a hunger
unacknowledged.

Luther in the Desert –

With this faith thou shalt mount up above and beyond the law, into that heaven of grace where there is no law nor sin. And albeit the law and sins do still remain, yet they pertain nothing to thee; for thou art dead to the law and sins.

Martin Luther
Commentary on Galatians

The desert teaches us to watch for mercy in the least likely places.

Belden C. Lane
The Solace of Fierce Landscapes

There seems to be the same difference between hell, purgatory, and heaven as between despair, uncertainty, and assurance.

Martin Luther
Thesis 16, *Ninety-Five Theses*

I

Black dream building and night conspired
                    my hands bled
from their braille search.
                              And then
you, Martin Luther, appeared
having got off at the wrong century
                    found the door easily
(you had been there before)

opened it, only
whites of your eyes available to light
and then — hell, purgatory and heaven, you said
not a desert —
your polite bow, Luther:
                    without an overcoat
                    dusting March snow from your shoulders
                    your long black shoes slippery
                              on stone.

2

Comforted in the arms of sleep
dear Luther
your conscience captive
to the word of God.

3

Again in the stairwell today
you descend the steps
      — that you would choose just now —

      eggshells opened
      cheesecloth limping to wrap butter
      black relief of flames eating cotton
      ashen flakes
      torn hair

Papists said
your mother
conceived of an incubus
his hoarse whispers.

4

Just past midnight, devil's pain
      there can be no anguish of conscience, no fear, no heaviness
falling
snow.

      Fire started in the middle of the cloth
      not along the torn edge, where you were bruised
      tearing yourself away, trying to be faithful.

Absence: embroidery, white on white.

5

— Everywhere white oleander blossoms, white vinca under
pines, none real, although not plastic. That these grow in a
desert, oasis notwithstanding —

6

Your theology students: their hearts lit like snow!
Free of Rome's tyranny, dead to the law
and to sin.

In the Mojave: rooftops prostrate themselves before mountains
like ideas of Jerusalem:

    a new and better Catholicism
stung by the tip of the Bible belt
abounds here —

    they baptize in fonts,
face the people, speak to children. If only
you could have seen this.

7

This, my Luther, is something that cannot be said clearly
there is so much in the way:

> a silence of palms
> pregnant with dark fruits falling
> mountains forbidding retreat
> smoky corners at the airport
> automated tellers spitting one hundred dollar bills
> fear of taking.

8

Always another chance, lies
coming out of another chance, this new world
disassembled.
You sacrificed everything so your prayer
might fly unmolested
blue and violet wavelengths close to earth.

You always assumed God believed
dear, dear Luther.

9

One hundred and seventeen degrees Fahrenheit:
not Jesus trying to walk on water —

      clumsy Joshua trees
      fall over in the heat
jealous godswater in all our bodies
conserves
against life's alternative,
even cactus jeopardized.

In full sun
neon mixes our tongues
      sun's wind gains redemption.

Flesh, A Naked Dress

The Orleans in the distance
throbs unashamedly
before the plummy mountains.

> Anabaptist rebels in Munster killed people guilty of sins:
> backbiting and complaining. They could not
> understand a city.
> They wanted to know
> where was God then?
> And then, who was the Lord?

The Orleans is Lord
for those who eat of its bread.

Strangers trim the palm trees,
the palms strangers too.

Miracle of the palms
profound
as a sea mount's trough,

undercurrent to glassy surfaces.

Mojave air evaporates all sea memory, dear Luther
palm's breath shortens thought, an odd circle
you could not have known, any more than a desert monk's purity
for which you prayed.

We pass over it.

I 2

By accident you say, your turmoil
projecting theology by accident much as the palm tree
throws itself to the wind, shedding glory to the ground,
open hands of God.
            Righteousness sweet.

A monk
by lightning strike:
work of Satan, your father said.

            By accident: the castle, monkish king with a queen!
New language, books written by you
fall from a printer's firmament, as you fell
into faith: diurnal shadow.

The day asserts itself, as the sun rises
falls, liminal times
casting rosiness upon easterly mountains
as if it remembers, as if it is a personal sun
as if the mountain too has faith.

Luther what accidental courage

            cold blood
stood in your way.

13

When I lived in a house that sighed
I took woodenness for granted.

Now that I live in a stuccoed fortress
I realize the hallowedness of trees

receive news in atoms of bristling air
all protection lies in prayer and

we are on the same earth
centuries apart, separated by more degrees than ever.

I am not in the second class of righteousness, prepared
to give my cloak away — oh no — I live in a fortress

protect myself from all things.

Evening primrose: a stout erect American herb.
What relation to the English primrose
whose jewel flowers shock, anticipating the pale yellow of
butter, plush basal leaves, green astonishment?
Evil resides outside this nursery where
a parrot talks to a child off school for Martin Luther King
Day. Evil rolls in the dust and in the nickels pulsing through
the city's capillaries, stupid machine-eyes click fruits and
numbers.

Primroses, inured to strobes and electronic noise in this plant-
hut, shock and confront my hypocrisy
— palest yellow.

15

Loyalty dents conscience: the heavy slap of pigeon flesh as it
ascends.

God made this land, they say, and because of you and your
darn *beruf* there are palm trees in this desert. Men from
Mississippi, fifty-eight this year, wear sweat shirts which
say *All gave some, some gave all* with a picture of four khaki
American boys carrying a fifth on a stretcher.

Luther: a white ceramic table dapples low latitude sunlight:
a long linen couch in silence: a lopsided bowl, empty: white
roses, armfuls.

Flesh, A Naked Dress

16

What's falling now will one day be fallen through

behind mob restaurants, crumbling university buildings
iron gates left opened.

             Unharmed
birds of the thirty-sixth parallel
scold busily at crime's neglect.
Pale trees fail the shabby patio
grackles challenge fallen life
larger than northern sparrows
whom a holy man
will notice

falling.

So far away from the light which we had in
common, the light that leaves shadow in the middle of things:
on tables, in corners, under trees. Instead a glistering mirage:
south.

       (And, O Luther,

           northern evenings ripped out of bright snow
           with only blue shadow left.)

    The wooden house:

                  concupiscence of the flesh
                  grief for its days
                  wrong as indulgence money.

One day the slightest kindness opens heaven.

An Event in the World

What does "really exists" mean? That they exist as
beauties.

Plotinus
The Enneads I.6.5

How to live in the body, comprehend God's rains
the ignored cornea registers:

> a pansy's purple, yellow
> play off green in the brain.

How to understand the clit, its sublime orchestration
> buttocks hinging the legs and paradise at once.

How to appreciate the belly's geography, its housing
> new countries in seminal dribs, amniotic sacs.

This is the problem of the body, how not to grieve
> inevitable loss: faith's too soon: a closed door
the world won't open.

*

Listen to the one who says: Why have they done this to me?
> embodiment's paradox
hunger.

*

Tree on the mountain grows gradually,
spruce in the Laurentides
shoots blue inches into the cosmos
penetrates mountain's stillness.

*

Egyptian women of the fourth century and all since:
know your mountains! You are wind and wood, eldest daughters

in separate booths. Your growing wood penetrates, you the apple
the tree, the problem, its knowledge —

chaste or no, the same desert. Christ's coming is a kiss
given or withheld: the same: you are guilty.

Small strengths the body knows, hide
from God's jealousy: leap into non-being.

This is sure: things have not changed:
my neighbour hungers.

*

Yellow falls into the eye like a book
from a high shelf, its brightness splayed:
right action.

*

This brightness clings, attaches to the All and One
like flame to poplar in a kitchen stove, burning poorly

after oxygen nothing

brightness buried in charcoal: porous result,
imperfect combustion: perfect rising from earth.

Flesh, A Naked Dress

*

If God only knew the trouble he's in:

the mind when it is looking out of itself to God
makes a simple vow, loves each cell into life
the Mind of All, loves it like a nursing mother the babe
whose mouth is greedy for goodness, its own, the milk
and hunger perfect chain of being

so the mind should be kept free
humbled as a mountain with a lake at its summit
stimulated by liquidity to know rain.

*

Gentle judgement: jolly her, make her laugh a happy daughter
shame on her embodied soul to judge and sweep the sky blue
tip the cosmic mixing bowl, pour and pour, begin
the ceaseless power of rain:

                              the desert
purifies, teaches the body: the heart
a book possible to read
when appetite for the Divine compels
happy action. Small. Begin.
Say it.

Notes

Desiderius Erasmus, Dutch theologian, wrote *The Praise of Folly* (*Moriae Encomium*), and dedicated it to Thomas More, his friend whose name was a source of the pun in the title. The character Folly talks about many fools around her and praises them for it. She calls wisdom foolish and fools wise. Of all Erasmus's writings, this has survived with the most appeal to a modern audience. He does not spare himself or his friends in his humanist satire. His "agenda," like that of his contemporaries, Thomas More and Martin Luther, was also church reform and rebirth.

In "Folly Laughs at the Bishop" Jesus's "one law" refers to Folly's chastising of the church hierarchy who assumed that the life of poverty and service, the law of charity, is for Jesus alone and for those who are less important than people of their own particular status, a sort of "leave that to the mendicants" attitude.

In "Joy of the Proper Tool," *adiaphoria* refers to a trance-like state brought on by fasting to the point of starvation. Italicized sections in "A Sometime Gravity" are from *Responsio ad Lutherum.* This text, written in 1523, was More's response to Luther in their intellectual "dog fight," which was characterized by theological and scatological invectives — in Latin, of course. The fight began with More's assistance to Henry VIII in his writing of *Assertio Septem Sacramentorum Martinum Lutherum* (*Declaration of the Seven Sacraments against Martin Luther*) for which Henry was named Defender of the Faith by Pope Leo X on October 11, 1521. Henry kept the title when he became the Supreme Head of the English Church in 1531. More was executed by Henry on July 6, 1535. Ironically, More was the real defender and Henry became the first English protestant.

Flesh, A Naked Dress

"Flesh, A Naked Dress" is based on my reading of Plotinus's relationship of the soul (she) to the Good (he) and the ascent of the soul. (For more, see *The Enneads*, Plotinus's life work.) The tiger, known as a predator and a fierce mother, is counterpoint to the lion, which became a Christian symbol for Jesus.

The italicized phrase in "Luther in the Desert, 4" is from Martin Luther's *Comment on Galatians*. The full sentence is: "Seeing then that sin has here no place, there can be no anguish of conscience, no fear, no heaviness. Therefore John says (1 John 5:18): "He that is born of God cannot sin."

In "Luther in the Desert, 15," *beruf* refers to Luther's theological stance, regarding the equality of secular and sacerdotal orders, a functional understanding of ministry and secular vocation which was one of the tenets of the Protestant Reformation.

KITTY WRIGHT

Susan Andrews Grace is the author of *Ferry Woman's History of the World*, which won the Saskatchewan Book of the Year Award in 1998, as well as *Water is the First World* (1991), and *Wearing My Father* (1990). A visual artist as well as a writer, she has exhibited her work in Canada and the United States, and worked as an editor and arts administrator for CARFAC Saskatchewan. She has taught creative writing at the University of Nevada and the Kootenay School of the Arts, and is presently on the faculty of the Oxygen Art Centre, *aka* Nelson Fine Art Centre.